Reptiles

Contents — **Page**

written by Pam Holden

Thousands of different reptiles are found in many parts of the world. They all have rough, scaly skin that feels like leather, with patterns that help them to hide from their enemies.

The scales are extra-thick pieces of skin made of tough stuff rather like our fingernails. All reptiles get rid of their outside layer of skin when the scales become old and worn out.

thorny devil lizard

3

Reptiles are cold-blooded animals that like to lie in sunny places to get warm. They don't make much noise – just squeaks and clicks and hisses.

Most reptiles lay eggs, then leave them to hatch. Baby reptiles have to look after themselves as they grow up. There are four main kinds of reptiles.

Lizards and snakes of all kinds belong to the largest group of reptiles, known as Squamata. They make their homes in trees, swamps, deserts, and caves in many countries. Snakes have no legs, so they move by sliding and slithering on the ground and along tree branches.

Some are quite small, but others are long and strong, with thick bodies that can squeeze animals to death. Some kinds are dangerous, as they spit poisons and bite. They eat eggs and animals, sometimes swallowing them whole! Snakes hiss when frightened or angry.

Lizards are fast movers that climb, jump, and run.
They live in trees, rocks, and underground to hide
from their enemies, which are hungry birds and
animals. They feed on fruit and leaves, or shoot out
their extra-long tongues to catch insects.

Most people know about an amazing lizard called the chameleon. If it gets hot or cold or angry, it quickly changes its skin from green to brown or gold.

Tortoises and turtles belong to a group called Chelonians, which all have a hard bony shell to protect their body from bad weather and hungry enemies. These reptiles look alike, but they live in different places - tortoises crawl slowly on the land, while turtles can swim far and fast in fresh water or the sea.

hawksbill turtle

Their food is different, too, because tortoises
eat grass, fruit, flowers, and vegetables.
Turtles feed on fish, insects, and water plants.

Crocodiles and alligators belong to another group, the Crocodilians. It isn't easy to see much difference between crocodiles and alligators. Both animals are long, fierce, and scaly, with sharp teeth and long, strong tails. Their home is in warm freshwater swamps, lakes, and rivers, or in salt water at the edge of the sea.

crocodile

Alligators and crocodiles are better parents than most other reptiles. After their eggs are laid, they cover them with leaves to keep the eggs warm. They stay near to their nests, to look after their eggs until they hatch. Then they carry their babies in their mouths to the water.

The fourth kind is the oldest reptile, the tuatara,
which lives in only one place in the world, New Zealand.
This unusual animal looks just like a small dinosaur.

It lives in burrows on small islands near the coast in New Zealand, where it is protected to make sure it does not become extinct. Tuataras have a third eye, and they often live to be more than one hundred years old!

Think about reptiles that live on Earth now and the dinosaurs that lived millions of years ago. What things are the same for both groups of animals? Can you name the reptiles that live in your country?